E. H. Geldard

FARR NURSERY

Hush, Little Baby

MARGOT ZEMACH

Hush, Little Baby

KESTREL BOOKS

KESTREL BOOKS

Published by Penguin Books Ltd

Harmondsworth, Middlesex, England

Illustrations Copyright © 1976 by Margot Zemach

First published in U.S.A. by E. P. Dutton & Co. Inc., 1976
First published in Great Britain 1976

ISBN 0 7226 5024 8

Book design and title hand-lettering by Riki Levinson

Printed photolitho in Great Britain by
Ebenezer Baylis and Son Ltd
The Trinity Press, Worcester, and London

For Auntie Rees of Crooms Hill Grove, London,
with our love

Hush, little baby,
Don't say a word,

Poppa's gonna buy you
a mockingbird.
If that mockingbird won't sing,

Poppa's gonna buy you
   a diamond ring.
If that diamond ring turns brass,

Poppa's gonna buy you
a looking glass.
If that looking glass gets broke,

Poppa's gonna buy you
a billy goat.
If that billy goat won't pull,

Poppa's gonna buy you
a cart and bull.
If that cart and bull turn over,

Poppa's gonna buy you
a dog named Rover.

If that dog named Rover won't bark,

Poppa's gonna buy you
a horse and cart.

If that horse and cart

fall down,

You'll still be the sweetest
baby in town.

Hush, Little Baby

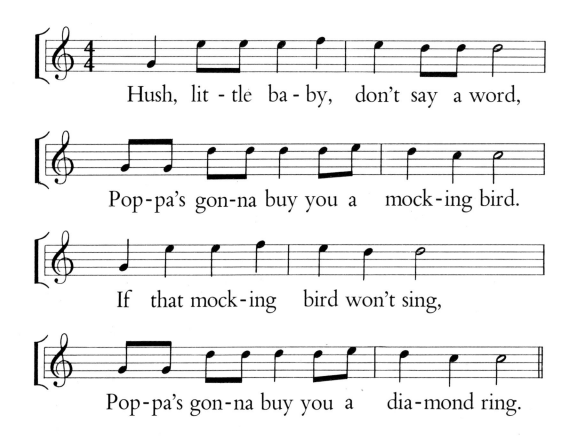

Hush, lit - tle ba - by, don't say a word,

Pop-pa's gon-na buy you a mock-ing bird.

If that mock-ing bird won't sing,

Pop-pa's gon-na buy you a dia-mond ring.

If that diamond ring turns brass,
Poppa's gonna buy you a looking glass.
If that looking glass gets broke,
Poppa's gonna buy you a billy goat.

If that billy goat won't pull,
Poppa's gonna buy you a cart and bull.
If that cart and bull turn over,
Poppa's gonna buy you a dog named Rover.

If that dog named Rover won't bark,
Poppa's gonna buy you a horse and cart.
If that horse and cart fall down,
You'll still be the sweetest baby in town.

MARGOT ZEMACH is the distinguished illustrator of many books, including *Duffy and the Devil* (winner of the Caldecott Medal), *A Penny a Look* and *Awake and Dreaming* published by Kestrel Books.

She says that she began to consider *Hush, Little Baby* a "tried and true" lullaby after singing it to her daughter Rebecca every night for a year and a half. During that time, the pictures of a large, untidy Mum, downtrodden, anxious Dad, and a squalling baby seemed to form themselves in her mind.

The artist and her four daughters now live in Berkeley, California.

The title is hand-lettering and the other display and text type was set in Griffo Alphatype. The full-colour illustrations were painted with tempera.